Sue Schott

Rachel
Schott

EVERYONE CAN BE YOUR FRIEND

by Sue Schott
illustrated by Rachel Schott

GLOBAL BLOCKS™

10121 Laurel Drive • Eden Prairie, MN 55347-3048

About the Author

SUE SCHOTT is the perfect person to write children's books. She is a mother and grandmother who loves children and loves reading to them. She believes that teaching children how to view themselves in a positive light is critical to their development and self-esteem.

Sue's background is deeply rooted in the values of small midwestern communities. She grew up in Early, Iowa and now lives on a farm in southern Minnesota. As a young girl, it never occurred to her that there was anything a girl could not do if she set her mind to it. In high school she was a cheerleader, yearbook editor, active in the French Club, and even played football with her brother and the neighbor boys on weekends. Sue attended Morningside College in Sioux City, IA and then moved to New York with her husband Lee.

After Sue and her family moved to rural Minnesota, she decided that the school board at her children's school needed a female viewpoint since there had never been a woman on the board. She was elected and served three terms, including 2 years as Chairperson. She made such a contribution that a local organization honored her with a plaque that said, "To Sue Schott, for Outstanding Service to HIS Community." The award had never been given to a woman before. She left the wording as it was and enjoyed the humor of it.

Sue writes the books from the heart. She feels the topics are "as important to children as their vegetables, but reading them should be as much fun as a trip to get ice cream." The other important aspect is that adults enjoy reading her books as much as the children enjoy hearing them read!

The wonderful characters in Sue's books are the creative work of Rachel Schott, Sue's daughter-in-law and mother of Sue's grandchildren. Rachel lives on a farm only two and a half miles from Sue.

Dedication

To my guys, Lee, Spencer, Marty and Britton who are gentle and kind and always there for me.
(Sue Schott)

For my mother-in-love, Sue, who believed in me and for Marci and Theresa and all your help.
(Rachel Schott)

Everyone Can Be Your Friend   Library of Congress Catalog Card Number: 95-79483   ISBN 1-885374-04-6

Toni was a turtle
who loved to run and play
along the path, inside the park,
she visited each day.

She often played
with Geri,
the giraffe,
her special friend.
They knew the
corners of that
park, the path
from end to end.

One day as Toni walked

　　along the lake beside her yard

a bully came up to her

　　and he pushed her very hard!

He told her that the park beside the lake

　　was just for him.

He didn't want her or her friends

　　to play or hike or swim.

Now Toni didn't like to fight, she much preferred to play.

So when she got away from him, she ran the other way!

He made her scared and made her cry. He didn't seem to care

that parks are put into a town for everyone to share.

When Geri came upon her friend
she noticed right away
that Toni didn't look too well,
her smile had gone astray.
"What happened to you?" Geri asked.
"You look
upset and sad."

"Oh," she replied,
"no I'm not sad.
I'm very
very MAD!

A bully tried to scare me

    and he did just that, you see.

I want to let him know

    he must not act that way to me.

He needs to learn a lesson

    so he won't be mean and tough.

He needs to know we all can play.

    This park is big enough!"

"Well," Geri said, "I know that you are feeling really bad.

     That great big bully scared you and you're looking awfully mad.

You're probably very angry and you want to hit him too.

     But if you go and fight with him, you'll end up black and blue!

To hit him wouldn't solve a thing and you would feel so bad.

We need to think of other ways to act when you are mad!

Of course you're feeling angry. You have a right to be.

But first,

go hit a pillow,

 stomp your foot,

yell at a tree.

Then later on this afternoon when all your anger's gone,

we'll meet again along the path beside the big park lawn.

Then when you feel much better, we will go back over there

and look for this big bully and we'll teach him how to share!"

"I sure don't want

to teach him,

I just want to

make him sad,"

said Toni,

and she made

her face look

very very

mad.

"Well," Geri said, "I know you think

     that bully's mean and bad.

But maybe he's just lonesome

     and he's really feeling sad.

He probably needs a friend

     or wants to play a game or two.

I wonder if he wouldn't like

     a friend like me or you?

I'm sure you'll feel much better

     when your anger goes away.

That's when we'll get together

     and we'll teach him how to play!"

So later on that afternoon when Toni went to play,

the bully waited in the park to make her run away.

But she stood fast, and looked at him,

    and then gave him a smile.

"If you would like to be my friend,

    it might be fun awhile."

Then Geri, Toni's friend,

    came out from hiding by a tree.

She stood beside the bully

    and he came just past her knee.

He looked at her and then he looked at Toni by his feet.

A sudden change came over him. He acted really sweet!

The bully changed expression, his scowl became surprise.

Maybe it was Toni's smile, or maybe Geri's size!

It really didn't matter 'cause

he said, "You want to play?

After all I said and did,

you'd like me anyway?"

He looked way up

at Geri's smile,

and down at Toni's too.

He hesitated, then he asked,

"Could I be friends with you?

My name is Alexander.

My daddy calls me Al.

But you can call me Allie,

if you want to be my pal."

Then Geri said, "We sure are glad that everything worked out!

'Cause sometimes there are bullies who just want to push and shout.

It's nice to TRY to be their friend, but some don't want to play.

Some bullies just won't ever change, so YOU must walk away."

Then Toni took Al's left hand
and Geri took his right.
They joined together arm in arm
and held on really tight.

The fun they had was better now
with three good friends at last.
And as they played that afternoon,
the time went by real fast.

"Oh boy," said Allie, "we can all be friends until the end!

And when we play together, EVERYONE CAN BE YOUR FRIEND! The playground and the parks are lots more fun with people there. The swings and slides and monkey bars are more fun when you share! If boys and girls can play there and it's safe for everyone, the park will be much better and we'll all have lots of fun.

We've learned
it isn't fun
to be so mean
and full of spite.

Just because
you're angry
doesn't mean
you have
to fight!"

THE
END

Look for other products by

GLOBAL BLOCKS™

"There's No One Quite Like You"

by Sue Schott, Illustrated by Rachel Schott
ISBN 1-885374-03-8

Self-esteem for children is the important message in this book! This is a story about Geri the Giraffe and Toni the Turtle, who find out the value of liking themselves as they realize that they have unique qualities and talents. The rhyming words and the bright colorful characters make learning a delightful experience! Children and the adults who read to them will love this book. $11.95, plus $1.80 s&h.

Flip*It™ **in Spanish**
ISBN 1-885374-02-X
Flip*It™ **in French**
ISBN 1-885374-01-1
Flip*It™ **in English**
ISBN 1-885374-00-3

Children have fun flipping the top half and bottom half of the pages to match over- sized numbers with vividly colored pictures. Learn colors and numbers in French, Spanish and English. Books designed by teachers for children 3 - 8. **$4.95 each** or $12.00 for all 3 Flip*It books, plus $1.80 s&h.

Geri and Toni Growth Chart

Have fun growing with Geri and Toni. Full-color chart measures to 57" tall. Spaces to insert pictures of your growing child.
$4.95, plus $1.80 s&h.

Global Blocks™ **- 30 hardwood blocks - in bright non-toxic colors.**
· In Spanish, French, or German.
· Learn a foreign alphabet.
· Learn 60 foreign words.
· Learn numbers 1 - 10, colors and shapes.
· Puzzle map shows continents and oceans.
· Be creative through manipulation of shapes.

$34.95, plus $4.50 shipping charge.

Parents' Choice Award Winner!

If your local bookseller or toy store does not have these items in stock, they can order them for you. You may order them directly from Global Blocks, Inc. for the listed price of each item, plus shipping and handling (s&h) for each item, but try your bookstore or toy store first.

Heaven Sent Creations
RR 2 Box 136
New Sweden, MN 56074
(507)246-5240

"Educational Toys and Books"